THE MIND AND ITS MEMORIES

C. B. Nordeman
1650 Beechwood Louisville, 4 KY

Auto-Biography
In part of the Author,

Published by

Nordy Press

Rome, Georgia

Mind and its Memories is dedicated to my Son and Daughter and to my four grandchildren and nine great grandchildren.

Someone has said Christianity can be condensed into four words. They are ADMIT, SUBMIT, COMMIT, and TRANSMIT.

I pray that all who read this booklet may comply to these four words in their Christianity. In these words are enveloped the message of the Church.

C. B. Nordeman

CONTENTS

PREFACE

C.B. Nordeman, my great grandfather, started writing his biography a number of times. My brother, C.B. II, and I each had some pages of those documents. I have attempted to bring those various typewritten carbon copies together into a unified document that describes his life in chronological order. This book tells the story of C.B.'s life as he recorded it. Sadly, it does not get into his personal life. It neither includes stories of how he met Ednah Dow nor any reference to his two children, Hoyt and Lois. It does underline how dedicated he was to the church and to his faith in God.

The addendums to this text are writings that were included in the typewritten pages. They were words of inspiration to him.

The pictorial family tree was added by the editor.

As he did, I dedicate this book to his descendants.

The process of creating this book has been challenging. Special thanks to my son Doug for his late night proofing. He helped me see the errors of wording and punctuation that I would never have found. He helped add clarity to the text. If there are still errors, they are all mine.

Dennis Nordeman

Charles Bernard Nordeman

INTRODUCTION

This is the life story of a boy now eighty years of age: just an ordinary boy, born in the humble home of Christian parents in a small county seat town in the southern tip of Illinois. It was a small town with a big name, "Metropolis," a name that is justified only by one of the world's largest cities in the northern tip of the [state].

Now, even though I am an octogenarian, I am still able to hit the keys and hammer out this message. I am sure I would have made my exit years ago, but as a shut-in He has kept me writing on the typewriter messages of comfort and cheer to other shut-ins. The year 1866 was the year of my advent. Naturally 1866 is my year. I was not conscious of it, no snap shots of what was going on in the world, but it was recorded and became history for me to read. I learned some interesting things. Of course I did not find these things during my infant years.

I found that communication had been established overseas, and the second cable was being laid crossing the Atlantic Ocean in 1866. I learned that a steam boat exploded on the Ohio River killing 100 people. I learned that a Farmer's organization was established and am told it is operating today.

1

The Russians, whom we today designate as Communist, this year or earlier sold us the territory of Alaska, price $7,200,000. It was called Seward's Folly, but it proved to be a gold mine.

1866

- Laying of the second Atlantic Cable.
- The Steamer Miami exploded on the Ohio, killing 100, The Missouri on the Mississippi, 156 lives lost.
- Fire destroyed 2500 buildings in Quebec.
- A farmers organization operating today was established, The National Grange.
- A Milwaukee printer, C. Latham Scholes, patented his typewriter.
- The Blacksmith was the hero of the trades and operated the service stations for local transportation.

1867

- The United States purchased Alaska from the Russians. People called it "Seward's folly," but it proved to be a gold mine. The purchase price of Alaska was, $ 7,200,000.
- Science research gave dynamite to man, developed first by Alfred Bernard Nobel, a Swedish inventor, who established "The Nobel Peace Prize."
- The Dominion of Canada was established.
- A hurricane of the Caribbean took 1000 lives and destroyed 150 ships.

1868

- The lawn mower was invented.
- President Andrew Johnson was impeached and acquitted.
- The year when Home and Family life was gathering strength in a nation of coming strength.

1869
- "Black Friday" when a financial crisis shook the Banks and financial structure of the country.
- Nevertheless, continued great progress prevailed and with it the completion of the nation's first Continental Railroad.
- The Westinghouse air-brake was produced this year.
- The first intercollegiate football game was played; Princeton vs. Rutgers, without radio. It was called "the year of beginnings."

1870
- Ground was broken near Duluth, Minn., for the construction of the Northern Pacific R.R., eventually to reach the Pacific Ocean.
- A Frenchman named Mege-Mouries produced what is known today as oleomargarine, an artificial substitute for butter. Did we hear something in Congress recently about this?
- The beginning of the Franco-Prussian war, the reverberations are still heard.

1871
- Prosperous and Disastrous.
- The great Chicago fire, caused by Mrs. 0'Leary's cow "kicking over the bucket." A blaze that swept more than 2000 acres and over 250 lives lost and 10,000 people made homeless.
- I saw this fire. I was five years old. At least I saw the reflections of the fire as elsewhere told. My first personal memory recorded event.

Up to this time transportation was not a whit better [than] in George Washington's day a century and [a] half before, or [even better than] in Julius Caesar's day.

3

I, like the rest of the Americans, begin to wonder, ask questions with an urge after the years of innocence, to play our delegated part upon the stipe of life and to play it well.

From this point on you will read some of my life stories brought back from the realms of memory. Not all of them. There are a lot I would forget. Just some high spots I give as a testimony, not of great achievement, but rather of righteousness (right living); a creation to help you, if you need help, whoever you are.

My memory holds things I can't forget, but thank God, He can. "Repent ye therefore, and be converted, that your sins may be blotted out." Acts 3:19.

I can't forget. God can and will if we repent and be converted.

1 A FAMILY IS CREATED

All my forebears in Germany are products of the land and natives of Germany. I make the statement, "products of the land," because I am told in their day, the land, be it small acreage or tracts of farming land, were designated a proper name. The tract my Paternal Grandfather obtained possession of was named "Nordeman." When my Paternal Grandfather moved in on it, his and his family name became NORDEMAN.

The same was true of my Maternal Grandfather Brockhaus when he obtained a portion of the "Brockhaus land." I cannot confirm this as truth, but as a boy, I was told it was an accurate fact.

The territory in which both forebears lived was [in Germany] near the Holland border line. I have not looked it up in the Geography, but I am told that Grandfather crossed the line into Holland to participate in the haying season.

My forebears' residence was in the little town of Osnebruck, Germany not far from Bremer-Haven, their nearest seaport, and near Hanover.

It seems there was quite a migration from Germany in the early eighteen-forties, and both the Nordeman and the Brockhaus families were bound for the "home of the free and of the brave," AMERICA. They came by ship, sail vessels, in those days. The Brockhaus family was among the first, the Nordeman family later. My Maternal Grandfather Brockhaus, his wife and two daughters, Anna and Margareth,[1] my future

Johann and Adelaid Nordeman
C. B.'s Grandparents

Mother, came first. As the ships were sailing vessels, their ocean experience was a long one. After weeks on the ocean, they arrived and settled finally in Cincinnati, Ohio. They arrived a good bit before my Paternal Grandparents did.

My Mother was then a two year [old] baby. She grew in the graces and liberties and benefits in the public melting pot of America.

She had finished the grade schools and arranged to become a companion to a wealthy woman on a trip by river to New Orleans. She began the trip, but just before reaching Vicksburg the boat caught fire. The husband of the woman to whom she was a companion took her to the top deck of the boat and told her to stand there until he called for her to jump. It got too hot. Afraid to stay longer and get burned to expected death, she took a chance and jumped. Just as she went over she heard the call for which she had been waiting. When she hit the water of the Mississippi, the man soon had hold of her and piloted her to the end of a log and told her to hang on. On the other end of that log was a big roustabout Negro, who, the day before, some women derided as being the dirtiest man they ever saw. Her feelings now were, would he shake her off of the end of that log? The passengers were all saved, but all Mother's belongings were lost. They had to be taken on to a slave plantation. The trip was not finished, and she went back to Cincinnati after financial adjustments were made.

There she obtained employment in a bindery of a publishing company that, at that time, was in the process of printing and binding a very large order of Adam Clarke's <u>Commentaries of the Scriptures</u>, four big volumes to the set, and here is a story.

I am looking at four of these volumes on my desk now. The pages have little rust spots on them that make them discards, but it does not in the least hinder the reading.[There were] little brown spots, a few on the page, but imperfect. What are you thinking? Is it "Be ye perfect as God is perfect?" Every time I see these spots the thought comes: AM I Spotless? White as Snow? Friend, there is such a thing as Christian Perfection. I did not intend to preach, but those are good thoughts to be thinking about and doing something about.

To finish my story, Mother saved all the culled or imperfect pages and with a few additional good pages, with the consent of the company, and a little additional cost, bound the pages into a set of commentaries. Mother sent them to me when I left home to hoe my own row. In passing I might say those books are within reach of my desk this moment

Now that I have that story off my mind, I will try to hitch on where I cut off, if I can.

My Paternal Grandfather and his family also left Germany later on. My father-to-be was a teenage boy and that family also settled in Cincinnati. My father-to-be did not have the opportunity to [go to] school but got his English by coming in contact with families to whom he delivered milk, he being a milk wagon driver, to American homes. He taught himself to both read and write in between times when he was not milking cows and driving a milk wagon in Cincinnati. German though he was, he did not drink intoxicants, even beer. He did not smoke or use tobacco in any way, and I never heard him swear. In fact, he was a German Gentleman: kind, affectionate and loving. It hurt him more than it did me when nightly for a while I had to go with him into the woodshed. Fathers spare the rod and spoil the child.

Both Maternal and Paternal Grandfather families were united in Cincinnati and lived there a long time. Finally they moved down "the Hudson of the West" and settled in Massac County of Illinois in a farming district known as the "Barnes." It was ten miles from the county seat, the town of Metropolis, a big name, but really a small village. The founders had an idea to match the extreme south with the extreme north of the state.

Grandfather Brockhaus' daughter married a farmer named Trampe. Her name was Anna, a sister of my mother-to-be. My mother lived with them a while.*[Editor's note: According to census records for Metropolis there was a Henry Trampe whose spouse's name was Anna. This might be the "Uncle Henry" that C.B. refers to later.]*

8

My Mother converted and became a Methodist while living in Cincinnati. Later in Massac County, the "Barnes" District, where my mother-to-be lived, there was a country circuit Methodist church and also a Lutheran church. They were within a couple of blocks of each other, with a joint God's acre, or burying ground, in between. My Father lived with the Brockhaus family who attended the Lutheran Church.

Grandfather's eye-sight having failed, they moved to Metropolis and built a home. Before the home was finished, a revival was held in the German Methodist Church on the circuit, in the country, and here is the story of Dad's conversion.

Henry Nordeman

In the first place, Dad was decidedly opposed to a Methodist mourner's bench. Moreover, he counted it as sacrilegious to shout in church. The joy of salvation in the emotion of gladness of spirit was nonsense, and he would have none of it.

9

He would accompany Mother to the church and sit on one side while she sat on the other. A rule prevailed in those days for the women to sit on one side of the church, the men on the other. WHAT A FOOL RULE.

The power of the Holy Spirit was present, searching the hearts of men. The preaching of the Word through the ministry of the Holy Spirit brought conviction for sin, repentance of sin and pleading for the grace of Jesus Christ. Many a shout was zooming the air in rejoicing because of sins forgiven. My Father came under conviction in spite of the fact that he had declared he did not believe in such "goin's on." To him it seemed foolishness. Then came forgiveness through Him who became the propitiation for sins and for the sin of the world. It is, in theology, the Doctrine of Regeneration, and it is what Jesus meant when he said, "Ye must be born again."

When that experience consummated in the mind as a fact, Father's soul illuminated with the fullness of joy. He became convicted and a pleading sinner for the grace of forgiveness. He surrendered shouting, arising from the altar, grabbing the preacher under his arm and sailed down the aisle of the church, happy as he had ever been before. He became a happy, free, glorious Christian and a Methodist at heart and in soul. Memory does not say whether they sang after this experience:

> "O' happy day that fixed my choice
> On Thee, my Savior and my God!
> Well may this glowing heart rejoice,
> And read its raptures all abroad.
> Happy Day, Happy Day,
> When Jesus washed my sins away."

10

Margareth Nordeman

My Father and Mother were married, and my Grandfather Brockhaus furnished the money that built the house in which I was born. The picture hangs in my room today. Come and see it. It was a Godly home.

In the meantime my Father learned the Cooper's trade.[2] Dad made barrels, flour barrels, but he drew the line on whiskey barrels. He said if they wanted to use them for whiskey, they had best not let him know it, and send the order through second hand for lard barrels. I guess that's one way of getting by. Dad said, "What you don't know, don't hurt you." True?

In my "little black book" I have this notation: Henry Nordeman and Margerita Brockhaus were married August 17, 1862.

Now we have a Christian husband and wife in their home in

Metropolis. The new home was built with the help of Grandfather Brockhaus. Now all are at home in the home built in Metropolis; the first sure symptoms of good minds, in health, rest of heart and the pleasure felt of really being at home.

A united Christian home was established with a Mother that was exceptional, facing the trends of the times in being set down as exceptional. I am glad of it as she was to be the trainer of my character, and I would need that as described in the following stray I recently picked up.

My Mother never smoked or drank
My Mother never swore;
My Mother never played at bridge
Nor counted up the score.

My Mother never plucked her brows,
Nor rouged her dear sweet face,
And on my Mother's loving lips
No stains of paint I trace.

My Mother never dyed her nails;
She never bobbed her hair,
But Virtue, Grace and Honesty
Have been her jewels rare.

Today My Mother could be called
Old fashioned well I know,
But, O how glad I am
That God had made her so.

Grandma Brockhaus and Grandpa were comfortably fixed. Their bedroom was a large corner room with their own four poster bed and crisscrossing rope around knobs on sides and ends, instead of modern mattresses and springs. Their door opened onto a porch at the end of which was the kitchen.

The adjoining bedroom to Grandma's and Grandpa's was that of Father and Mother. The third in the row was an extra room for company later on. It was not dignified by any other name, only as "the front room."

Birth place of C.B. Nordeman Metropolis, IL 1866

Across the hall were two rooms to be rented out to help defray expense of living, and later on for family use if necessary.

The lot consisted of about an acre on which Grandfather cultivated a large garden, and enough hay was raised to feed two cows all the winter.

"Home Sweet Home,
Be it ever so humble
There's no place like home."

Happiness, rest and love, but the greatest is love.

13

2 AN EARLY ARRIVAL

My brother John Edward was the first addition to the family, born August 7th, 1864. But the Heavenly Father evidently wanted to make sure that the new family should be represented in Heaven. Therefore he called little boy Edward home on May 15th, 1865. "Suffer the little ones to come unto me, for such is the Kingdom of Heaven."

My advent into the world was not to be the "first born" but the "only son," and my advent was April 10, 1866.

They say that all the days of my active life were exemplified in the matter of my advent; hurry, impatience, never still for one moment, on the go, the future view resonant with activity and glory. They say I was not slated to make my [debut] on the scene until the middle of May or early June.

But I was here and observing that the WORLD was not ready for me. I went to sleep to wake at the registered hour.

I realized when I opened my eyes that the fact was that the world was busy on my behalf. In this year of 1866, the first paper from wood pulp was made. That was natural, or else how could this new message be publicly publicized?

Without paper how could I survive? Without paper what good would a typewriter be? But, thinking along with God, I found that God in his goodness put into the heart of a Milwaukee printer, C. Latham Sholes, to invent a typewriter, and he did. The typewriter and paper and I have become loyal friends.

The blacksmith was the hero of the age in 1866 when the machine was coming to power. Who was more in demand than the blacksmith to shoe horses, to mend broken tires on wheels, wagons and buggies? Had I been a mature man in 1866, I'm sure I would have been a blacksmith.

As the months went on so also did I, but my place on [the] stage of action was yet to come. Mother and Father were still members of the little Methodist Circuit Church in the country. The Preacher visited us quarterly. In fact, our home was headquarters for the class meeting of Metropolis members.

On one of the Preacher's visits, it was decided I was to be baptized. The Preacher's name was Hankemeyer, and he was German in thought and language. Mother told him my name was to be Charles. The Preacher started to baptize me Karls, but she interrupted him and said, "NO, I said his name is to be Charles." The Preacher tried again, but the best he could do was CHARLESS, (with the emphasis on "less"). My Mother's Father's name was Bernhardt. Mother insisted later on that I, in writing my name, for the middle letter just use "B," or use as my middle name BERNARD. So you note my Mother was acclimated to the American way of life.*[Editor's note: In various sources C.B.'s middle name was spelled Bernard, Bernhard, and Barnard. I'm not sure which is correct.]*

This town had, at the time of my adolescent period, four churches of which Methodist was the oldest and largest. All the social life of the town centered in and around these churches.

It was a town supported largely by farmers in the county and, by the way, it was the smallest county in the state. There were no modern made roads in those days that ran according to section lines, no automobiles. A two mule team jolt wagon was the conveyance of the farmer to take him to town, which as a rule took an entire day to complete.

There was no railroad. I did not see a locomotive or train of cars until I was seventeen years old. My first introduction to them was in Cairo, Ill., when as a member of the state militia, I went to camp in Springfield, Ill. That was the outside environment of my early teenage years.

Now for a peek at influences within the inside of that environment:
> A Mother's love begetting love.
> Winning extreme affection.
> The only comforter and consoler.
> The teacher of prayer and petition. "Now I lay me down to sleep."
> "God bless us everyone."
> Mother the source and dispenser of all wisdom.

At five years of age I was permitted to defer retirement until Father read a chapter from the sacred word, and all the family knelt in prayer led by Father. Often I fell asleep on his knees and failed to hear the amen.

The next influence in my career was Sunday school attendance; the Presbyterian in the morning, the Methodist in the afternoon. I treasure the book entitled <u>RAM KRISNA PUNT,</u> published in [my] birth year and given to [me] by [my] Presbyterian Sunday School teacher, Miss Scott. Mrs. Dr. Bronson was always the ideal of womanhood in my mind. Her influence still abides. The [book is about] a Bengalese boy, his starving, suffering, [and] the cholera epidemic. It developed in me a missionary spirit that is at high pitch at eighty years.

A little later came the experience of attending services in the Metropolis church, sitting together in a pew, the whole family. It was the mandate of Father and was not to be disregarded.

Disciplinary rules obeyed were forming habits that were calculated to develop and abide.

There is a quotation that goes something like this, "Sow a thought, reap an action; sow an action, reap a habit; sow a habit, reap a Character; sow a character, reap a destiny." The quotation may not be verbatim correct, but it is true and it was evidently the under principles of my Mother and Father.

3 SCHOOL DAYS

School Days, teen years, grammar grade, had their influence on me. Three score years ago school session was opened with the singing of a gospel hymn, reading a chapter from God's Word and a prayer offered by the Teacher, or the Lord's prayer recited by the pupils. Most of my teachers were professed Christians and members of the church and were interested in spiritual as well as secular education.

Metropolis had no high school, and as far as college, I scarcely knew what the word signified. I have learned since the exceeding great value of an education obtained in a Christian College. Though I did not have college training yet, paradoxical as it seems, I was for some years a member of the Board of Trustees of Union College, Barbourville, Ky., and was Secretary, Vice President, Treasurer and finally, for several years, President of the Board, a service of half a century. On retirement [I was] awarded the title of "Member Emeritus." I signed many college diplomas, yet never owned one myself.

I began school life in the German Lutheran church, a temporary arrangement while the new school building at Third and Metropolis streets was completed. My teachers were Mrs. Daily and Mrs. Lute Ward. The church was on Ferry and Sixth St. I afterwards finished all the seven grades in the new building.

I did have a little more than a seventh grade training in Metropolis. There is a rather long two story building on the N.E. corner of Sixth and St. Catherine streets. I think that is right. It belonged to J. F. McCartney, a leading lawyer and citizen of the town. A Mr. Thomas blew into town and rented it and opened a pay school, called a seminary.

Seminary Building during the 1937 flood.

Somehow he did not last long, and he turned his lease (I presume he had a lease) to a Professor Kerr, who had recently with his family become citizens of Metropolis. I remember their boys: Bart, Glen, and George, and come to think of it, there was a younger boy whose name I cannot recall. But George and I came to be close friends, and also later on in Louisville.

Prof. Kerr took charge of the school. I understood it was a school of higher learning, and some of the seventh and eighth

19

grade pupils attended for they did now have an eighth grade in the Public Schools. In addition, quite a number of out of town students attended. I concluded I would attend, being able to afford it, because of money I earned working on a farm and at the Spoke Factory of Yost Bigelow and Co.

It was called a Seminary because they told me that was the first step to college. I knew naught about college, but I got some information all in a lump when my Grandfather explained to me that, when I became old enough for college, he would provide for me the same as he had for my cousin Ella. She had been provided the funds to attend a college at Mount Pleasant, Iowa.

Grandfather passed on in 1883 when I was 17 years old, and in the shuffle of his affairs, I was not afforded the privilege of his promise.

But I do want to give one more story of my SEMINARY days in Metropolis.

When the seminary opened up, I was one of the first to enroll, along with some of my public school associates and quite a contingent from the county and even some from other points in the state.

The school, or rather the Seminary, enjoyed a freedom that was enticing. Behavior depended on honesty of judgment instead of rules. There was a desire to achieve within the bounds of good fellowship. Rhetoric, philosophy, and penmanship were not known to the most of us and inspired a venture in connection with our studies. My time in the so called Seminary was under the tutorage of Prof. Thomas and a Mrs. Daily, the latter being of great encouragement to me. I well remember a time when, discouraged with failure, she put her arms about me and said, "Charlie, not failure, but low aim is crime." I shall never forget these days at the so-called Seminary. They were the high lettered days of youth.

A Herculean Literary Society was organized into classes of exhibitions to give entertainment to the public on the first Monday of each month. How I enjoyed the Herculean Literary Society meetings. I was one of the stars of that organization, playing the part of the persecuted Dutchman in Comedy, Spartacus in tragedy in his address to the Gladiators in Capua, and Shylock, a Jew, in the Merchant of Venice. These gatherings were the life of the town. The meeting was to be held in the Christian church just across the street on the opposite corner. This was the event of the town, and the attendance was the indicated appreciation of the public. The students were divided into three sections of six performers, three ladies and three men, each triplet to perform once every three weeks.

My team was No. 1. My partner [was] Miss Myra Wilson, the Methodist minister's daughter. We officiated for several months, and the weekly presentations became the social events of the town.

I recall one of our presentations. I declaimed the "Spartacus address to the Gladiators," and my partner chose "Whistling in Heaven." I cannot recall just who the other two teams were in our section, but I can say our efforts were applauded, and thanks and congratulations were offered. We were adjudged the winners. My father was present, and he received many compliments on the presentations of his only son. That, I am sure, puffed me up to unmerited worth.

That evening in escorting Miss Wilson home, we were two happy youths, and the road home was altogether too short.

An entrancing, beckoning, shimmering, infatuating call seemed to inspire me to aspire to one of three obligations for my life; the ministry, the law or journalism, and many were the predictions I would be a preacher.

Those Herculean Literary days were the one thing, outside the regular church services, for the people of Metropolis of that day to look forward to in expectation.

Charles Bernhard Nordeman
as a teenager

There is just one thing I was about to forget. Miss Myra and I were section one winners for the evening, and that has been a beautiful memory even to this day. I met Miss Myra many months, yes years afterwards, in Chicago, and our memories naturally centered on the good old town of Metropolis on the banks of the Ohio, "The Hudson of the West."

4. CONVERSION

"Of all the memories solemnly stored away;
awake but one and lo' what myriads rise,
while others fly away."

Just now an outstanding memory pushes to the front and will
not [go] down, claiming to bear witness to man's greatest asset
as he enters life's careers, an experience called conversion.

My Uncle's family had announced a friendly family gathering
on a certain night, and we were invited. I [believe], however,
they would have been much surprised if we had shown up.
The lines were quite clearly drawn those days between the
Methodist and the Lutherans, especially the German
Lutherans, but I personally wanted to go.

As usual I went with my Father to prayer meeting on
Wednesday night. The meeting was routine, songs, prayers,
exhortation on the word of God, and sometimes testimony, all
as usual, except that as we knelt to pray, I fell under
conviction of sin. When we arose from prayer, I alone
remained on my knees. I prayed, they prayed, we all prayed.
We sang, and the whole tenor of the meeting was changed.
"Will he pray through?" "It all depends upon his complete
surrender," said the Preacher. I did not pray through.

23

The Holy Spirit convicted me of sin of which I repented. God, for Jesus Christ's sake, forgave my sin after which came the witness of God's spirit to my own spirit that now I was an adopted child of God. I could truthfully say, "I know whom I have believed." There was not even a shadow of doubt. No "I hope so." No guess about it. I had experienced regeneration and been born again, converted. That was a "constantly abiding" experience to be followed by a growth in grace of our Lord and Savior Jesus Christ.

The HOLY SPIRIT, administrator of the new life, had spiritual gifts to bestow "dividing severally as he will" as recorded in 1 Cor. 12. The real meaning is that faith saves you, but that it takes works to keep you saved. Each person has some talents, and these are to be expended in work of "Evangelize or die."

The night of the party came. Mother's position was, "If you go, it is without my consent." I did not go. Had I had the same regard for God as I had for my mother, my trouble would all have been over. The Preacher said, "My boy, it is up to you now to work out your own salvation."

"How?"

"By confessing Jesus Christ as your Savior, testifying to that in prayer meeting, feeling or no feeling."

That made me REMEMBER my little black book and its clipping there right to the point involved. It reads like this:

> "Three men were walking on a wall; FEELING, FAITH and FACT. FEELING got an awful fall, and FAITH was taken back. FAITH was so close to FEELING, he

fell too, but FACT remained and pulled FAITH up and FEELING TOO."

This little scrip is exactly my experience.

I remembered the Fact that "God so loved [the world] that He gave his only Son that whosoever believeth should not perish but have ever lasting life." When Faith took hold of that fact and accepted it, JOY, unspeakable and full of glory, filled the heart and witnessed that now the life was "hid with CHRIST in GOD."

5. PROVIDENCE INTERVENES

For two years I worked on a farm at $8.00 per month and board, and with the money thus made and saved, concluded it was high time to get out and get on my own.

When Grandpa Brockhaus died there was some question [about] where he kept his valuable papers. Uncle Henry, Ella's father, and my father were indebted to Grandpa Brockhaus for loans made to them to build their homes. They wondered where Grandpa's papers were so they could settle the estate. I heard them talking and I said, "I know."

Uncle Henry said, "What do you know?"

I said, "Go into his bedroom and I will show you."

They went, and I pulled the last bureau drawer out on the floor. I reached in and pulled a copper box secreted between the bottom of the bureau itself and the bottom of the drawer itself. I used to pull it out for him when he wished to examine his papers. The result was that it proved Uncle Henry had paid the loan to him. Therefore, the balance of Grandpa's estate, after paying my Mother her share, left nothing to the promise

26

to me that was to have [been] my chance to go to COLLEGE. "ALL'S WELL THAT DOES NOT END WELL." The world moves ON.

Later on when I was preparing to go to Louisville, he [Uncle Henry] said to me, "Well, I expect to see you walk back the long road home. Maybe the persimmons, strawberries, peaches, and apples will be ripe to help you along." That was not poetry, not even cheap sarcasm. Then Christmas came. I mailed him a Christmas present of a Gillette razor. Who am I to sit in judgment?

I do not intend to portray an autobiography of my own life beyond my existence in my home town. That was a period of about seventeen years. At this date, to inventory the days of the remaining seventy years would possibly be interesting, but it is really another story.

The flood of the spring of 1884 was an experience of suffering to many. Our home was involved to the extent of five or six inches of water on the floor. I remained in the home the last night and the next morning stepped out of my bed into water on the floor, and it was in February at that.

Father's custom "City Mills" was wrecked by high water and a cyclone visit. Bank failure concluded the tragic picture.

Severing the home ties is not pleasurable, especially to those who are breaking ties for the first time. It not only affects the one leaving, but the ones left behind.

It was a desperate situation to add to the family troubles, and in no way could I help except to exit myself out of the situation. Why stay amid that wreck and ruin? But where to go and what undergirding did I have to venture on? Well, there was a Christian home, a family altar, a mother's special prayer, a memory of a good Sunday school teacher, a church with its sacraments and a dear old preacher, the Rev. C. P. Wilson. He was interested in me because we were both named Charles and both akin to Charles Wesley through our earlier brother Jesus Christ.

My further undergirding was the clothes I wore, a few extras, and $24 [from] three months wages on a farm. With these assets I concluded to make a venture into the future. Where? Chicago? Cincinnati where I had kinfolk? Where?

Mother taught me when you get in a jam and can't see the way out, to pray about it, and pray I did. The answer came clear.

News came to town that a new boat was coming up the river, the Steamer DeSoto, on her maiden voyage to Cincinnati. That decided the question. To Cincinnati we would go. I had the prospects of at least a two weeks visit with relatives and free board while looking for a job.

The Steamer DeSoto on which I came to Louisville in 1884

I would get on the DeSoto, which was to land at the wharf in Metropolis tomorrow evening. Fortunately, I had enough money to pay my fare to Cincinnati. To this, Mother agreed.

I spent the night restfully, for my mind approved my action. My girl too approved that I was doing the right thing and promised to be at the boat tomorrow evening to see me off. The DeSoto was a new boat, and this was her first trip. I leave to your imagination all that happened the next day waiting for the boat. I heard the citizens collected a crowd to board the boat and have a dance on the way to Paducah, twelve miles up the river. The boat arrived about 11 P.M. I spent the better part of the evening with my girl. Then we were off with banners flying amid the music and the dance to be repeated all along the way to port.

I knew the Ohio to Paducah and did not retire until after we arrived there, some twelve miles from my home town, but on the Kentucky side of the river.

There was so much stir going on, I had no time to get lonesome. When we got to Paducah, I went to my stateroom and to bed and finally went to sleep, the boat still in port at Paducah wharf.

The DeSoto lay at the wharf at Paducah until early morning when the half dozen couples from Metropolis left the Desoto to return to Metropolis by the regular daily Paducah and Cairo packet. They had made the trip for the dancing privilege afforded into the early morning hours.

Breakfast, and then off on another jaunt up the Ohio River with fare paid to Cincinnati, the river low, the weather warm and travel slow.

I was aboard one of the finest Ohio River steamers, my fare paid to Cincinnati, Ohio. I did not know when I would get there, but notified my relatives I was on the way and that it was not necessary to meet me as I had their address.

The river was at low stage, it being in July 1884, the 10th day or rather night. When the boat was on her way, breakfast was announced. My berth was near the bow of the boat, and it was a good thing I asked if I was to sit at the table in the front. The waiter told me, "No, that's the table for the Master, pilot, clerks and other officers of the boat."

I was glad I asked the question and thereby saved myself some embarrassment. I was told to go down to the cabin to the third table. So, when the time came to go, I was just as sophisticated and knew my manners as well as any of them. The meals were good, and now the question of how to put in the day. A chair on deck was an opportunity to view a constantly changing scene of beauty.

There lived a citizen, well known and prominent in Louisville, named Will S. Hays, a famous song writer who pictures the Ohio River in verse titled, "The Hudson of the West." For your entertainment and pleasure I insert it here.

"The Hudson of the West"
Will S. Hays
The Ohio River between Cincinnati and Louisville

When the lips of summer kisses
Nature in her sweet repose,
And the dew drops kiss the faces
Of the flower and the rose
And the nightingale is singing
To his mate upon her nest,
Silence sits upon the bosom
Of the Hudson of the West.

30

See the pale moon in her beauty
Float into the world of space
And the grand old hills throw shadows
As they hide before her face
Shadows lay like curtains
Softly on the river's breast
Adding beauty to the grandeur
Of the Hudson of the West.

There the lovely hills and valleys,
Clothed in robes of verdant green,
And the forests, fields and hillsides,
Lend their beauty to the scene.
Here a mansion, there a cottage,
Then some lovely vale of rest
On the banks of the Ohio
On the Hudson of the West.

Here a pretty little city
Or a place of some renown;
On the hillside sits a village
In the valley rests a town.
One unrolling panorama
Nature furnishes the guest
Of the steamers of the Mail Line
On the Hudson of the West.

See the grand, majestic steamers
On sweet nature's looking glass
Mirrored in their speed and beauty,
In the moonlight, meet and pass;
There's a thrill of joy and pleasure
Leaps into each human breast
As we view the scenes enchanting
On the Hudson of the West.

31

I have personally been on the Hudson, and Will Hays did well in paying this tribute to the majestic Ohio.

At that time in 1884, I think I am correct in saying there were no dams in the Ohio and no locks, except at Louisville. At the present time there are, I am told, some forty or more dams and locks making year round navigation possible. Our travel was slow. The pilot was constantly seeking the channels deep enough to float the boat. Many hours of the day and night we could hear the cries of measuring depths of water from the bow of the boat in words like these; "mark-twain, quarter-less-twain, four feet," as they were cried out by the mate at the prow to the pilot in the pilot house.

At three points on the river we got stuck on a sandbar. After bells forward and bells backward, the Captain permitted a goodly company of us to take [a] yawl, or small boat, and go out on an island of sand to the Indiana side of the river with the instructions that, if the whistle blew, we were to hurry back aboard to resume our journey. We spent some three hours on our improvised picnic, made acquaintances, and had a good time.

[Editor's note: Bell signals were used on steamboats to communicate between the pilot house and the engine room. The Pilot would pull cords in the pilot house to ring bells in the engine room. One bell would mean forward; two bells reverse. Orders could also be communicated through the speaking tube.]

We spent three nights and four days on the "Hudson of the West" and arrived at Louisville on the morning of the fourth day, entering the canal early in the morning. It was a new experience to me to be on a boat that was raised from one level to another by the opening and closing of great gates.

[Finally] the closing of the last gate floated us out on the upper river level above the falls.

Coming out of the locks, we soon came to the Louisville Wharf on the morning of July 14, 1884. We ate our breakfast on the boat and were told we would lie at anchor at the wharf until 12 o'clock noon, and all who desired might go into town, see at least a part of the city, and shop, meaning window shopping.

I did not finish my trip to Cincinnati, Ohio because God intervened.

It was a respite, and all took advantage of the privilege of doing some sightseeing. I preferred to go it alone, walking out Fourth Street, the main retail street, some three blocks and then following, shall I say, an urge or lead, a divine one as it proved to be, to Floyd Street where I learned the L and N depot was moving properties to Tenth and Broadway.

I mused around there a bit, interested in what was going on, then resumed my walk on Jefferson going as far as I saw the cross street sign [that] read Hancock Street. I concluded to go on Hancock to the next street which I noted was called Market, thinking I would go down that street. When I reached Market [at the] corner of Hancock, I noticed a church on that corner, quite a large church. I read the sign board: "First German Methodist Church, Rev. H. G. Lich, Pastor."

The words startled me. Why, in all this busy, big city, must I go direct air line to this church? The name "Lich." I knew him well. What was happening? It meant something, but what?

The parsonage was next door. I went to it, rang the bell and the preacher himself answered.

"Dr. Lich, I am sure glad to see you again so unexpectedly."

His brows knitted but he evidently could not place me.

I said, "I gave up my bed for you and slept on the floor. You were our Presiding Elder the first time I saw you. I remember I took you to where my Father worked. I remember you talked German to me, and I felt all the way to the factory you could not speak English. I tried so hard to speak high German and [was] used only to low German. What a struggle, and how your heart must have chuckled at my poor effort that I was making."

The Doctor smiled, then laughed heartily. "Charles, is it not? Son of Henry Nordeman? Come sit down. Let us talk of those days. I remember. The memory has been stored away but now leaps into action and tells me how crestfallen and surprised you were that day when I greeted your father in English and told him of your efforts at German."

We talked of Father and Mother and of some members in Metropolis that I knew, and then he asked me where I was going and how come I was in Louisville? I told of the flood, the loss of the mill, and my expectations of going on to Cincinnati at noon to get a job and free board for a couple of weeks. He said, "Why not get a job in Louisville? I'll help you get one."

I was startled. "Suits me. I believe I would like it," I said.

Does prayer change things? Has Mother's prayer changed things? She did not want me to go to Cincinnati to my relatives where they served beer at meals.

I went to the boat, got my belongings, and Bro. Lich got me a job in a hardware store at $3.50 a week. Board $2.50, surplus 50 cents, but I was a citizen of Louisville.*[Editor's note: I'm not sure about C.B.'s math but that is what he typed.]*

"Prayer changes things." When I wrote Mother about it, she wrote back, "God answered my prayers, prayer changes things."

I was now in the city where the Methodist Episcopal Church South was organized in 1844. The German church alluded to heretofore was the Methodist Episcopal Church. Because of my friend Rev. Lich, I united with that church, although I would have appreciated a fellowship with an English church.

Soon after entering the employ of George Welstein, a member of the German church, [I was] going down a street on an errand for my boss. I noticed a sign on a door of a building that read, "Wanted: men to unload schooners." Well, to a country boy in a crowded city, the word schooner meant a boat, and to the country boy it meant that men were wanted to unload boats. I went down a few blocks to the river to see what the character of the job was and what [was] the pay.*[Editor's note: A schooner is a type of sailboat but it is also a large beer glass or a container for holding liquids while drinking.]*

I met a policeman and asked him where the schooners were. He looked quizzically at me and said, "What schooners?"

I said, "The ones to be unloaded."

He laughed and said, "My boy, they are on every corner. Pass 'em up, kid. They are no good. They begin with beer, but they soon get to whiskey and the workhouse."

The light broke in. Beer? Whiskey? Unload? The country boy in a crowded city understood the item. It was stored in the mind, and for the first time in years, that item of memory jumped out to get into this story. Total abstinence is the only safe rule. I practiced that and gave many prohibition addresses in Kentucky and Indiana for the Anti-Saloon League, of which Dr. N. A. Palmer, D.D. was Supt. in Kentucky.

I stand in memory at the grave of one about my age, a little younger maybe, who died of delirium tremens, and I was like John Wesley. In the same situation as I, he said, "But for the grace of God's saving power there lies John Wesley." No wonder that during the Murphy meetings in days gone by, as men signed the pledge, [you could hear] the volume of "Amazing grace, how sweet the sound, that saved a wretch like me." I am glad I did not get to my river journey's end, for temptations awaited me there. "God works in mysterious ways, his wonders to perform."

The retirement of Dr. Lich from the pastorate [occurred] on a Sunday in September, 1886. On the first Sabbath of the new Pastor, the Rev. J. Reid Shannon D.D., I united with Trinity M. E. Church. Even now I hear him announce his text, "Have ye received the Holy Ghost since ye believed?" Strange that in all of the sermons I ever heard, memory brings forth this text and Dr. J. Reid Shannon.

I was living in a boarding house and now working as clerk in an office as a collector, clerking auction sales. I received a letter from my old home town pastor. He had learned from Mother I was back in the English Church. He said,

> "You are now in a great church listening to an
> able and a great preacher. I am still in this
> small town and need your help. You hear great

preachers. I hardly ever do except when I go to Annual Conference. You can help me preach better if you will. Won't you sit down Monday mornings and write me the text of his sermons, the outline of the sermon, such of the outstanding points he made. If the sermon is printed in the Monday papers, cut it out and send it to me. I can use any special sermonic material. Your Mother says she has prayed you through and will continue to do so. Affectionately, C. P. Wilson."

After I had done thus weekly for a year or more, it dawned on me, in the language of Mark Guy Pearcrat, "catching them with guile." Rev. Wilson, the home town family pastor, was influencing me to attend church regularly and to get out of the sermons more than I ordinarily would. It was not a help to the pastor but instead helping me, and it paid dividends both ways. Pastors in rural sections have a large responsibility in seeing to it that boys leaving rural homes are safely housed in the church in the urban communities. The Christian influences impress, develop and abide in time and eternity. My prayer at eighty years is:

> Let my mouth be filled with thy praise
> And with thy honor all the day
> Cast me not off in the time of old age;
> Forsake me not when my strength faileth.

Brother Wilson's request and memory advises that the notes on the sermons are in a book and still in my possession.

If only preachers realized their great opportunities of stabilizing the boys leaving the small town church for the big city.

I think this story, told years later to Dr. Wilbur F. Sheridan, gave him the conception to preach a sermon on "A country boy in a crowded city," which on request was thrice repeated.

[Sheridan] was a true Christian, a great preacher, and as pastor of Trinity preached to S.R.O. crowds. The altar, filled with a penitent response, was rather a usual and not just an unusual thing on Sunday nights.

The following week after I became a member of Trinity, Dr. Shannon visited me where I was employed and said he was anxious I should become a subscriber to the Western Christian Advocate, now the Christian Advocate. As I write, that was sixty-four years ago, and I bear testimony that the reading of that paper weekly has been of great help to me in my Christian experience.

John Wesley's motto, "The world is my parish," became to me a challenge to greater missionary effort on my part through Trinity Church. Until now I am known as the Mission friend in India. As Chairman of the Committee of Missions and Church Extension for over a score of years, I have been instrumental in building a Church center and parsonage in Tanger Deacan, India, and $300 annual support of a hospital health center in the jungles at Yallery, South India.

I have had the extreme glorious privilege of having Bishop Chitamber, now deceased, Bishop S. K. Mondol of Hyderabad, India, and the Rev. Marlsippa David, District Superintendent at Tanger, all Hindus, in my home. What a blessing to affiliate with them in Christian fellowship and to realize that someday Jesus shall reign where the "sun does his successive journeys run; His kingdom spread from shore to shore, Till moons shall wax and wane no more."

Soon after becoming a member of Trinity, the denomination organized the Epworth League for its young people. Trinity's' young people switched over from Christian Endeavor [to Epworth League] by one vote. I was elected its first President. I had become acquainted and had gained favor in the eyes of the people and from time to time was elected Sunday School Supt., a member of the Official Board, a Steward, and I was in deed and truth in fellowship with Trinity folk.

I frequently was called upon to lead the prayer meeting service, and, to my surprise, was invited to make the annual Epworth League address at the morning church hour. In other words, I was to supply the preacher's sermon time. This was one of the hardest things I was called upon to do. I had spoken in public at prayer service, but to stand behind the sacred desk, well, I needed to think about that. Yet I was told it was the unanimous request of the League. I took the request and invitation under consideration for a week.

I prayed about it, searched for a subject I thought was appropriate, and in my personal devotions that night I read Isaiah 29. The 6th verse caught my attention, at least a part of it that read, "Israel shall blossom and bud and fill the face of the world with fruit." What a text of promise. Is not Israel the church of God? Is not the Epworth League the blossom of the church, now budding, and soon to flourish, the fruit to the glory of God? Yes, I accepted the invitation and I preached that Sunday morning. Preached, yet not a preacher, and yet with power and uplift of vision to my own soul. I felt I had done the unusual for me, and the service left a prevailing spirit of "Look up and Lift Up."

Within a few weeks, at the next District Conference, I was licensed as a Local Preacher in the great Methodist Church. The license is securely fixed in my Bible, a Bible presented to me by the Epworth League of Trinity through my esteemed brother and friend, Chas. C. Stoll on August 7, 1892. It is in this paper you will find my first license to preach, authorized July 29, 1893. [It was] signed by E. L. Shepard, President.

I still have some of those old sermons, especially the "Blossom, Bud and Fruit" one. But the first sermon I preached and really called a sermon, inefficient as it probably was, is on this text:

> "For as many as are led by the Spirit of God,
> they are the Sons of God." Romans 8:14.

As I read these sermons over occasionally, I wonder how I dared to write and preach them. Yet, they were the presentation of fundamental truths, and I confess as I read my simple utterances, God's blessing was in them.

6 STEPPING STONES

It was not my intention to remain in any one job long but to use it only as a stepping stone to a better one. My education was limited to grade school and a semester of seminary course. I must learn as I went along. While I was clerk in Capt. Irwin's office, Assignee of Trust Estates and Bankruptcies, I studied the books of the various concerns coming into our office. I traced bookkeeping entries until I obtained quite a good idea of bookkeeping and learned this one definite fact. In double entry bookkeeping, "Every debit must have its credit, and every credit its corresponding debit to carry on balanced bookkeeping." I therefore felt justified to reply to a want advertisement in the daily paper reading, "Wanted: a young man to keep books for a Manufacturing firm. For information write N. Fury, care Victoria Hotel, 10th and Broadway, City."

In a day or two I received notice to call at the hotel for an interview with Mr. Fury. My interview consisted of a quiz, my age, background, church affiliations, and how did I happen to choose to come to Louisville? When?

I told him the whole story as related herein. He seemed to

enjoy it and, when I said I was a Methodist, he remarked, "A Wesleyan 'eh? Well they are emotional Episcopalians here but a branch of Church of England," but it seemed to please him.

The consummation was, "I do not think you know all that is to

C.B. Nordeman

be known about bookkeeping, but what you do not know, I do know, and I feel you have in you the making of a bookkeeper. Come down to the factory, Tobacco Manufacturing, on Monday morning, 8 o'clock, and I will see you started, salary $662/3 per month."*[Editor's note: The salary is reproduced here the same as the original document. I leave the interpretation to the reader.]*

I was there on the next Monday morning and was introduced

to the old bookkeeper who was being transferred to the Chicago agency, but who would be there to help me for several days. The first thing I was put on to do was to find the balance. Trial balance was out 10 cents. I had not seen a trial balance book. I did not know what a trial balance was. I was on fire inside. I lifted a prayer, "O' God, stand by, move me to be calm, guide me what to do."

He, the old bookkeeper, left me. Thank God he went out and stayed all day. I noticed that the difference between the debit and credit on the Ledger was set down accordingly on the trial balance book, likewise on the trial balance book either debit or credit. I was on my way and began to check each account. It was not more than an hour or two until I found a column in which, upon addition, there was a difference of 10 cents. Mr. Fury, coming out of his office, asked what I was doing. What should I say?

"Hunting balance," I said; "Here is something I have added several times and get different answers."

"Let me see," said Mr. Fury. "Maybe the posting is not plain. Where is your day book? Let's look up this posting. Here it is," he said. "The posting should be $42.00 and it's $42.10. Change that and you have your balance."

The next morning when the old bookkeeper came in, all of us being present, he asked me, how about trial balance? To my joy and everlasting gratefulness, Mr. Fury answered, "Mr. Nordeman found where you had posted wrong to the amount of ten cents."

During my first year with the Foree Tobacco Co., there came many times when I was puzzled with and about entries, but I said nothing. I came back after supper to the office and, taking out old records and searching and finding comparative conditions, worked them out, always remembering to ask God's help and always remembering to thank God for his help before closing the office and going home.

I was with that firm I think eight years, until they sold out and quit business.

In writing these true little stories, I have learned through experience that God is your wisest Counselor. He is "Our refuge and a present help in time of trouble."

When one memory or series of memories has passed across the stage of remembrance, it is a problem to choose from the many who appeal for presentation. The one making the most earnest appeal just now is part of the following story.

It is hard to recall dates, and they are not significant anyway. It's enough to say this story is in the realm of politics that ends with a religious experience. That abides even to this day, yet culminated a half century ago.

Mr. H. H. McCulloch, a member of a large Baptist church, won the election as Tax Receiver, but to qualify he had to put up a Bond of $250,000. Of that amount, $150,000 had to be a Trust Co. Bond and $100,000 an approved personal bond.

Mr. R. R. Clover of my church, Trinity, agreed to sign that bond providing he would be allowed to name the Cashier and Chief Deputy (one person) for the Tax Receiver's office. Without my knowledge or consent, Mr. McCulloch's Bonds and my nomination as Chief Clerk and Cashier were confirmed by the Board of Alderman, and I became a politician and a city employee.

I felt elated at the news of my employment and found that my two friends, Chas. C. Stoll and Al Rentlinger, were largely responsible in seeing that Mr. Glover's choice of Chief Clerk and Cashier were carried out.

In certain seasons, tax paying time, allowing discounts, we handled fortunes in cash. The balance of the seasons [we were] checking up delinquents for others to collect. We had alarms of all kinds in our office, or the buttons rather, that set off the alarm in the Police Dept. in the building. But bandits did not bother us, whereof I was exceedingly thankful to Almighty God.

Here is a sequel to this Revenue cashier job, and memory clamors for the write up, so I feel maybe it best to tell the story.

7 EPWORTH

The unfolding of that story is still, after half a century, in the minds of quite a number of living persons.

My pal in Trinity Church was Frank S. Coon. He had been a teacher of the teacher training class when I was superintendent of the school. He was an absolute dependable, optimistic soul. Both of us had bikes and often rode to the city outskirts viewing the landscape o'er. On one Sunday afternoon we rode into a settlement south and adjacent to Louisville. We came to M street and Fourth. In front of M Street was a large block, no dwellings or buildings of any sort, but there were a host of children playing on the commons, gathered from the neighborhood. [There were] many men coatless, without collar or necktie, lounging. Some were drinking beer, despite the fact saloons in those days, not cafes, were supposed to be closed on Sunday.

Frank said to me, "C.B., don't this look like a prospect for a Sunday School?"

I said, "Let's find out."

We obtained the attention of the children, chatted with them, and asked if they went to Sunday school. Some few said they did, but the majority said they would. On the spur of the moment, we said there will be Sunday school out here in the open unless, during the week, we could find a hall. We talked with some of the men, and nearly all agreed it would be "a great thing for the kids."

On L at the north end of the block, we found a two story building, store on first floor, and a hall that would seat 75 people on the second floor and available for Wednesday and Sunday nights. The other nights, at the time, were taken by the A.P.A., the "American Protective Association," that secretly flourished in those days. On my enthusiasm and Frank's optimism, we rented that hall believing God would help us do a good work.

We distributed hand bills all over South Louisville about the Sunday school at Elks Hall the next Sunday. Now, a problem arose, as they will do. We needed chairs, benches or seats of some kind on which the kids could sit. But where to get them? Trinity maybe? Hope so. To Trinity we went and found none available. What now? Well, first of all, Frank and I had a prayer meeting and laid our problem upon God. But still, we considered every possible solution, but didn't get anywhere.

We were so enamored in our project, we just couldn't believe in failure. We were anxious, but we determined to have Sunday school next Sunday if everybody had to stand up. We both somehow jumped this text at each other, "Be still and know that I am God."

Thursday morning Mr. McCulloch came into the large office, called me into his private office and unfolded this story.

"C.B.," said he, "I am in a dilemma. I wonder if you could suggest a way out? You know I am Sunday School Supt. at 22nd and Walnut Baptist Church. Well, I am also a sort of general manager down there. In our basement we have stored a lot of benches, and we need the space for coal. The question is, can I sell those benches? Can I rent or loan them? Can I find storage for them? Now, can you suggest anything?"

I was flowing over, filled to the brim, hardly able to speak, but I managed to say, "Brother Mack, you are an answer to prayer."

"What do you mean?" he asked.

I told him the whole story in detail. He listened and said, "You know the old hymn says,

> 'God works in a mysterious way
> His wonders to perform.
> He plants his footsteps on the sea,
> And rides upon the storm.'

"You have my authority to lay off today, find yourself a truck, go down to the church, load those benches, take them to your mission. Use them. They are yours."

We did. When the job was done, we had exactly enough benches to leave a nice center aisle. There was not a surplus bench. One more would have been one too many.

We were ready for the M Street Sunday School next Sunday. They came and grew in numbers, the Epworth League of Trinity helping.

To do effective work we needed larger quarters. The attendance grew steadily. We began a night service in which

Brother Coon led the singing, and I tried my best to do the preaching. The attendance increased until we had to put out the S.R.O. sign. Oh how we wished for a larger room.

A few Christians from out in the country on the Circuit found us. Their experience in life, prayer and song was a big help, and generated itself into a desire for a protracted revival meeting.

They wanted to know if we could have a two weeks meeting. I told them we would see what could be done. I called on our Pastor at Trinity, and he agreed to give us two weeks of preaching of four nights each week, saying he would be compelled to reserve Wednesday nights for his own Trinity prayer meetings.

In as much as I had already gone through preaching to them as best I could a number of Sunday nights, I felt that Brother Coon and I could carry on the Wednesday evenings he could not be there. The only fear I had was that the four nights [Bro. Turner was a guest preacher] would so charm the people that the Wednesday nights, when we were left alone, would fail in numbers and enthusiasm. But that old, optimistic Bro. Coon said, "I do not know one note from another, but I know every song in the song book. Now I'll be the singingest evangelist of all time, and I can get people to sing. You are not a preacher like Turner, but you get your preaching rules from him. Remember, 'begin low, go slow, add the fire, wax warm and sit down in a storm.' You preach the Savior Jesus. I will be the singing evangelist. You be the preaching evangelist. God must do the rest."

That meeting opened with a preparatory service on Sunday night with Brother J. W. Turner, pastor of Trinity, in charge. On Monday the people came. All could not get in the building.

Standing room was all taken. Monday and Tuesday were omens of what was to come. Wednesday, Bro. Coon sang and I preached. It was a good meeting, but I did not have the gift of foresight to see that Brother Coon and I would have to go alone the rest of the way. Dr. Turner had made his last appearance. He was called to Indiana on the account of the severe illness of a member of the family.

It seemed, henceforth, I had to do the preaching. Brother Coon and I had a prayer meeting, and, as a result, decided to carry on, God helping, onto victory for the remaining days.

We began the altar call that Thursday night. The old mourner's bench had kneeling penitents, and so it went into the next week. As you know, I was employed in the Tax Receivers office during the day, and after closing hours I prepared my sermons, if sermons they could be called. Anyway, God blessed His Word, and we went through another, or third week, and had some score conversions, some reclamations and an undergirding to build a church. This one thing was proven to me in that meeting, viz: that "Faith will save you, but it takes work to keep you saved."

We now had faith enough to aspire and go to work to see about building a church, and determined then and there, when built, it would be named Epworth Church.

The growth of Epworth Mission was recognized by the Quarterly Conference of Trinity Church. All who joined the church at Epworth Mission were enrolled as members of Trinity, until a church building to be known as Epworth Church could be erected, and the Mission members of Trinity could then be made into a congregation of members of the new Epworth Church.

A lot for the new church was obtained, located at M Street near Fourth. Through the kindness and the generosity of friends and South Louisville people, a Chapel was built at a cost of about $2600.00.

Let me quote from a book entitled After Thirty-five Years, A History of Trinity Church. Quote:

"The Mission in South Louisville was organized into Epworth Methodist Episcopal Church, and so approved by the Quarterly Conference of Trinity Church, which finally resulted being recognized as a separate charge by the Presiding Elder.

"The new building was duly dedicated. C. B. Nordeman was appointed preacher in charge until Conference, and the Conference at the next session, and for the year ensuing appointed C. B. Nordeman supply Pastor. So, Epworth was launched out on its own."

These two years in their own house of worship was a period of ingathering. A Woman's Missionary society was organized, a weekly night prayer meeting established, a new and better church school organized, a financial plan set up, and a salary set up for the preacher (all of which he donated for the purchase of lights and supplies). Electric lights had not invaded South Louisville at that time.

Those almost two years, as a Pastor of a flock, ministering to them and trying to expound the scriptures to them as best I could, were red letter periods in my life. I occasionally visit the little church which has a splendid organization, a very fine pastor, a good parsonage, is self-supporting, and pays its apportionment in world service. As I say when I visit there, I am pleased to have them honor me as founder and Father of their Church. My only regret is that my co-laborer, Bro. Frank Coon, is not here to enjoy the experience with me. He has translated from the Church Militant to the Church Triumphant.

Epworth is self-sustaining and contemplating a new location and a new Epworth with new quarters with all conveniences for effective service.

There are some good sports at Epworth. I am lifting "A Good Game Guy's Prayer" for them. It was lifted by Ted Sanford for his Kentucky athletes from the Chaplain's Digest. I pass it on to the Good Guy Sports of Epworth.

"A Game Guy's Prayer"
Dear God: Help me to be a sport in this little game of life. I don't ask for any place in the line-up. Play me where you need me. I only ask for the stuff to give you 100 per cent of what I've got. If all of the hard line drives come my way, I thank You for the compliment. Help me to remember that You won't let anything come that You and I together can't handle. And help me to take the bad breaks as part of the game. Help make me thankful for them.

And, God, help me always to play on the square, no matter what the other players do. Help me to come clean. Help me to see that often the best part of the game is helping the other guys. Help me be a "regular fellow" with the other players.

8 FINAL REFLECTIONS

May I say I began in Louisville on a wage of $3.50 per week, just as an unknown. I held, as time went on, better and larger positions. Memory insists the [highlight was the] position I had with J. M. Robinson Norton and Co. as Credit Manager for ten years. It was an honor and gratifying to me to see that business grow and multiply itself six times while I was there. The credit loss during the period of my credit managing was only about one tenth of one percent. The Company concluded to liquidate.

I was favored by being offered a position with the Credit Clearing House of New York as Manager of the Louisville office. I later transferred to the Chicago office where my wife was seriously ill with the "flu." After a two year service in Chicago, we moved back to Louisville. My wife had a hard time in recovery, but did, and soon at this writing we will celebrate our sixty-first wedding anniversary.

In coming back to Louisville, I became a Board Member and Secretary of the Inter-Southern Life Ins. Co. I merely mention these facts to show what can be done. Being a country boy, who believed in God, in prayer, and got joy in service, I always believed, "God is our refuge and a present help in time of trouble."

Yes, God has blessed me abundantly, and the Church has honored me beyond my deserts.

Ednah and C.B. Nordeman

I was a member of the Board of Trustees of Union College, Barbourville, Ky., and was Secretary, Vice President, Treasurer and, finally for several years, President of the Board. [It was] a service entire of half a century, and on retirement [I was] awarded the title of "Member Emeritus." I signed many college diplomas, yet never owned one myself.

C.B. Nordeman at the Credit Clearing House

The Church honored me with my election as Lay Delegate to the General Conference held at Saratoga, N.Y. in 1916. I was a member of the first jurisdictional Conference of the South Eastern Jurisdiction of 1940 in Asheville, N.C. I was many times a delegate to the Kentucky Annual Conference and to the Louisville Annual Conference.

If I remember correctly, I was a member of the Board of the Methodist Deaconess Hospital some 22 years and its Treasurer 16 years.

In the matter of politics, I grew up a Republican. My first recollection of a political campaign was the campaign of Grant and Colfax. My father had erected a flag pole in the front yard and bought me a flag and a streamer with the name of Grant and Colfax printed on it. I remember pulling the flag and streamer to the pole's top and discovered I had the streamer on upside down.

My first vote was cast in Louisville for "Rum, Romanism and Rebellion," James G. Blaine, by viva voce vote at Eighth and Green Streets. In those days I felt politically lonesome in Kentucky, as lonesome as I have felt in later days when voting prohibition. Of all the Presidents of my time, I revere the Quaker Christian Herbert Hoover. Derided, vilified and denounced by the Democrat Party, but like the Savior, "he answered not again," but went on serving and made one of the greatest come backs of all time. Even the opposition party drafted him to outline and draw plans for the economic and successful operation of the government.

This about takes in my span of life. I have allowed memories, at least those that highlighted the years of my life, to be mentioned as my mind poured them forth. Many I have rejected as being of no significance, and some memories must be buried in my own mind forever. They should have never become memories.

I began this writing with "Remember now thy Creator in the days of thy Youth." That I did, and the years have gone by, and I have had pleasure in them. It has not always been "sunshine and roses."

I have experienced suffering, illness, and four times on the operating table. At one time the situation was so serious my Pastor announced that he thought I would be in Heaven the next Sunday. While I failed often to live up to my high privileges in Christ Jesus, My Lord, his forgiveness and merit availed for me, unworthy as I was, and I recovered. God's mercy and goodness have followed me all the days of my life in my adopted city of Louisville.

I have been blessed far beyond my deserts. From a pittance of $3.50 a week and a bare living, I "increased in favor with God and man" and advanced step by step, as recorded in this autobiography. I felt constrained to tithe my income from the time I was earning the sum of $1000 annually up to $5000 annually, my highest achievement.

I have proven God's promise as regards the tithe [to be] true all together. Out of my nine tenths savings, I acquired my own home all because I remembered my Creator in the days of my youth. All my family, wife and son and daughter are alive and are all Christians, and death has not entered our home. I am glad and thank God.

I would like to live my life over again. Of course that cannot be. But at my age, 84, (quoting John R. Mott at 83 in Amsterdam), I am beginning to sense the fact I have another life to live, and, by reasonable calculations or expectations, I shall begin it before many more months.

Three things I have learned, three things of precious worth, to guide and help me down the western slopes.
- How to Pray and Toil and Save.
- To Pray for others. To receive whatever comes to me, divinely sent.
- To Toil for universal good since thus and only thus can good come unto me.

CELEBRATING 60 years of marriage are Mr. and Mrs. Charles B. Nordeman, 1650 Beechwood. Both shut-ins, they expect only a few close friends to drop in to see them on Sunday, the day after their anniversary. March 1949

Footnotes

1. C.B. states in the family tree document that Margaretha was a cousin to his father.
2. C.B. states in the family tree document that his father "was a cooper by trade but for many years was foreman in the plow handle dept. of Yost Biglow & Co. He later operated the City Flour and Feed Mill which was destroyed by the great flood of 1884."

APPENDIX A
OLD AGE PRAYER AND COMFORT

Psalm 71

9: Cast me not off in the time of old age; forsake me not when my strength faileth.

12: O' God, be not far from me: O' my God, make haste for my help.

14: But I will hope continually, and will yet praise thee more and more.

17: O' God, thou hast taught me from my youth: and hitherto have I declared thy wondrous works.

18: Now also when I am old and grey headed, O God, forsake me not? Until I have showed thy strength unto this generation, and thy power to everyone that is to come.

20: Thou, which hast showed me great and sore troubles, shalt quicken me again, and a halt bring me up again from the depths of the earth.

21: Thou shalt increase my greatness, and comfort me on every side.

24: My tongue also shall talk of thy righteousness all the day long: for they are confounded, for they are brought unto shame that seek my hurt.

Psalm 73

26: My flesh and my heart faileth: but God is the strength of my heart, and my portion forever.

I agree with John S. Roberts, who protests he is "Not Growing Old."

NOT GROWING OLD

They say that I am growing old,
I've heard them tell it times untold.
In language plain and bold,
But I am not growing old.
This frail old shell in which I dwell
Is growing old, I know full well,
But I am not the shell.

What if my hair is turning grey?
Grey hairs are honorable, they say.
What if my eyesight's growing dim?
I still can see to follow Him
Who sacrificed His life for me
Upon the Cross of Calvary.
What should I care if time's old plow
Has left his furrows on my brow?

Another house, not made with hands,
Awaits me in the Glory Land.
What though I falter in my walk?
What though my tongue refuse to talk?
I still can tread the Narrow Way,
I still can watch, and praise and pray.
My hearing may not be as keen
As in the past it may have been,

Still I can hear my Savior say
In whispers soft, "This is the way."
The outward man, do what I can.
To lengthen out this life's short span,
Shall perish, and return to dust,
As everything in nature must.
The inward man, the Scriptures say,
Is growing stronger every day.

Then how can I be growing old
When safe within my Savior's fold?
E're long, my soul shall fly away,
And leave this tenement of clay,
This robe of flesh I'll drop and rise
To seize the "Everlasting prize,"
I'll meet you on the Streets of gold,
And prove that I'm not growing old.

Victor Hugo sums it all up this way. "When I go down to the grave, I can say like many others, 'I have finished my day's work', but I cannot say 'I have finished my life.' My day's work will begin again in the morning. The tomb is not a blind alley. It is a thoroughfare, it closes in the twilight, and it opens in the dawn."

APPENDIX B
BODY, MIND AND SOUL

The writer of ECCLESIASTES begins, (12) "Remember now thy Creator in the days of thy youth, while the evil days come not, nor the years draw nigh, when thou shalt say, I have no pleasure in them."

He is writing to the creature of the Creator. That means you and me and all of us. Who is the Creator? Of course it is God.

We humans are of the animal kingdom, but superior to all other animals in that GOD made man of the dust of the earth and then breathed into his nostrils the breath of life, and man became a living soul.

Out of the dust of earth he made man's body, the flesh, bones, blood, muscle and nerves. In other words, the house or temple in which our mind and soul lives.

Was it not John Adams who was asked one day in his old age how he was getting on and replied, "Well, the house I live in is going into decay and wearing out and soon I will have to move out, but as for John Adams, he is alright and ready to move into his new home."

Yes, the body will return to dust, but the mind and soul will return to God who gave it. You can read about it in the second chapter of Genesis.

THE MIND

Now what of the mind? We all know we have a mind, and we are exhorted to "let this same mind dwell in you which was also in Christ Jesus." So, therefore, the mind must be resident in the body.

Milton says, "The mind has its own place, and in its self can make a Heaven of Hell, and a Hell of a Heaven." Mind is a kingdom. From it come ideas gathered and stored for weal or woe, for good or evil.

Mind is the gathering place of our will concept, the storehouse of our thoughts, thinking after God or stocked up from the Devil's inspiration against the will of God.

What a responsibility we have as to what we allow in our minds. It is the one place where memory dwells, stored away.

"In the Pleasures of Man" the poet Rogers puts it this way.
"Lull'd in the countless chambers of the brain,
Our thoughts are linked by many a hidden chain.
Awake but one, and lo! What myriads rise?
Each stamps its image as the other flies!"

In our minds is where the storehouse of memory is, and this storehouse is ample to hold the "Remember thy Creator in the days of thy Youth" and through all the days until the "Conclusion of the whole matter."

The Destiny of the Soul.

Man, like God himself, is a mystery. God is Triune, "Father, Son and Holy Spirit." Man is a trinity also, body, mind and soul.

Dr. Ridout asked in one of his sermons, "who can understand that strange mysterious thing we call the soul?" Science cannot explain it. Evolution is in the dark about it. Psychology claims to know it, but knows it not!

The soul is that mysterious something that God breathed into man's nostrils and man became a LIVING SOUL. It is the divine in man and is immortal. The soul is man's most valuable asset.

APPENDIX C
DISCIPLES PRAYER
THE LORD'S PRAYER FOUND ON BATTLEFIELD

Note: This prayer composition, into which a now unknown Author uniquely fitted the Lord's Prayer, was found on a battlefield of the War Between the States. The date is July 4, 1863. It was first printed on heavy satin, and has been reprinted by various newspapers, first by the Denver Post.

> Thou, to thy mercy seat our souls doth gather to do our duty unto Thee

Our Father

> To Whom all praise, all honor should be given for Thou art the great God

Which Art in Heaven

> Thou, by thy wisdom, rulest the world's whole frame, forever, therefore

Hallowed be thy name

> Let never more delay divide us from Thy glorious grace but let

Thy Kingdom Come

> Let Thy command opposed be by none but Thy good pleasure, and

Thy will be done

> And let our promptness to obey be even the very same

On Earth as 'tis in Heaven

> Then for our souls, O Lord, we also pray, thou would'st be pleased to

Give Us This Day

> The food of life wherewith our souls are fed sufficient raiment, and

Our Daily Bread

> With every needful thing do Thou relieve us and of Thy mercy pity

And Forgive Us

All our misdeeds for him whom thou did'st please to make an offering for

Our Trespasses

And for as much, O Lord, as we believe that Thou wilt pardon us

As we Forgive

Let that love teach where with thou dost acquaint us to pardon all

Those Who Trespass Against Us

And though, sometimes, thou find'st we have forgotten this love for thee, yet help

And Lead Us Not

Through soul or body's want to desperation nor let earth's gain drive us

Into Temptation

Let not the soul of any true believer fall in the time of trial

But Deliver

Yea, save them from the malice of the devil and both in life and death, keep

Us from Evil

Thus pray we, Lord, for that of thee, from whom this may be had

For Thine is the Kingdom

This world is of Thy work, its wondrous story to thee belongs.

The Power and the Glory

And all Thy wondrous works have ended never, but will remain forever and

Forever

Thus, we poor creatures would confess again, and thus would say eternally

Amen

APPENDIX D
HELPING OTHERS

You who have read so far will observe I emphasize prayer because in my own experience, what success I have had along religious endeavor, has been through prayer.

"Silver and gold have I none," but out of my spiritual wealth and experiences, I have given to others, and that is saved throughout all eternity.

C. D. Meigs has expressed this ideal of laying up treasures in heaven through service and for others in this prayer.

Lord help me live from day to day
In such a self-forgetting way
That when I kneel to pray
My prayers will be for OTHERS.

Help me in all the work I do
To ever be sincere and true
And know that all I do for you
Must need be done for OTHERS.

Let "self" be crucified and slain
And buried deep and all in vain
May efforts be to rise again
Unless to live for OTHERS.

And when my work on earth is done
And my work in heaven begun
May I forget the crown I've won
While thinking still of OTHERS.

OTHERS, Lord, yes, OTHERS,
Let this my motto be.
Help me to live for OTHERS
That I may live like thee.

My soul rejoices this morning that memory persists in crowding to the front with the adventures and efforts made for God and the building of the Kingdom of our Lord Jesus Christ. There is value, imperishable value, that cannot be lost like some material values that once were but are no more.

APPENDIX E
THE NEW ERA

In the new era just about to dawn, after a great revival shower of "Holiness unto the Lord" and through the out pouring of the Holy Spirit, men and women will vote as they pray.

It will be an era of righteousness (right living). The door to that era is beginning to open now.

The "Baptism of the Holy Spirit," fitting men and women for that new era, is conditioned upon obedience. It means entire surrender of one's will to God, ourselves, and all we have

a) TO GO, where He wants us to go,
b) TO BE, what He wants us to be,
c) TO SAY, what He wants us to say,
d) TO DO, what He wants us to do.

ARE WE ABLE to cooperate in bringing the church on the advance for the reign of the Prince of Peace?

HERE IS WHAT IT TAKES
1) To differ without complaint
2) To endure without breaking
3) To be forsaken without forsaking
4) To give without receiving
5) To be ignored without grieving
6) To ask without commanding
7) To love despite misunderstanding
8) To turn to the Lord for guarding and wait for the awarding.

In the approaching era, no atom or H bomb will serve, only an advance from Goodwill and Brotherhood and Righteousness.

APPENDIX F
OBEDIENCE

I do not know who wrote the following verses on "Obedience." Shall we choose the easy way, or shall we follow the voice of the Master?

OBEDIENCE

I said, "Let me walk in the fields."
He said, "No, walk in the town."
I said, "There are no flowers there."
He said, "No flowers, but a crown."

I said, "That the skies are black,
There is nothing but noise and dim."
And He wept as He sent me back
"There is more," He said, "There is sin."

I said, "But the air is thick,
And fogs are veiling the sun."
He answered, "Yet souls are sick
And souls in the dark undone."

I said, "I shall miss the light,
And friends will miss me, they say."
He answered, "Choose tonight
If I am to miss you, or they?"

I pleaded for time to be given;
He said, "Is it hard to decide?
It will not seem so hard in Heaven,
To have followed the steps of your guide."

I cast one look at the fields,
Then set my face to the town.
He said, "My child, do you yield?
Will you leave the flowers for the Crown?"

APPENDIX G
PRAYER

Prayer is the burden of a sigh,
The falling of a tear,
The upward glancing of an eye,
When none but God is near.

Prayer is the simplest form of speech
That infant lips can try,
Prayer the sublimest strains that reach
The Majesty on high.

Prayer is the contrite sinner's voice
Returning from his ways,
While angels in their songs rejoice
And cry, "Behold, he prays."

Prayer is the Christian's vital breath,
The Christian's native air,
His watchword at the gates of death,
He enters heaven with prayer.
O' Thou, by whom we come to God,
The Life, the Truth, the Way,
The path of prayer Thyself hast trod,
Lord, teach us how to pray.

How often have I uttered that last verse and had my soul filled
with prayer and exultation of Jesus Christ, my Savior, Lord
and Master.

APPENDIX H
PICTORIAL FAMILY TREE

Leonard Milton Dow
B. Dec. 30, 1805 in Salem N.H.
D. Dec. 23, 1875 in Hampton, N.H.
Married Rebecca Milliken

Their second child was Charles LaFayette Dow.
He married Mary Katherine King March 20, 1861.

Charles LaFayette Dow
Father of Ednah Dow

Mary Katherine King Dow
Mother of Ednah Dow

B. May 23, 1834 Portland, ME   B. Jan. 22, 1840
D. May 1923 Louisville, KY   D. Dec. 3 1911

C.B.'s Grandparents

Johann Heinrich Nordeman   Adelaide Dulman
B. Feb. 10, 1804 Osnabruck   B. May 24, 1802
D. March 5 1895   D. Aug. 1872

Their second son was John Henry Nordeman

C.B.'s Parents

John Henry Nordeman
B. Aug. 6, 1838
D. May 18, 1902

Margaretha Elsabine Brockhaus
B. Jun. 21, 1831
D. Sep. 4, 1919

They were married Aug. 17, 1862
They had two sons and three daughters.

John Edward
B. Aug. 7, 1864
D. May 15, 1865

Charles Bernard
B. Apr. 10, 1866
D. Nov. 19, 1957

Margaret Alice
B. Jun. 23, 1869
D. Aug. 27, 1944

Emma Florence
B. Nov. 29, 1872
D. Jun. 26, 1873

Laura
B. Aug. 16, 1874
D. May 30, 1906

Charles Barnard Nordeman
Charles Bernard Nordeman
Charles Bernhard Nordeman
C.B. Nordeman

Ednah May Dow   Charles Bernard Nordeman
B. May 18, 1867   B. April 10, 1866
D. March 31, 1952   D. Nov. 19, 1957

They had two children:
Hoyt Vincent
B. Jan. 7 1891
D. Dec. 2, 1951

Lois
B. April 25, 1898
D. March 21, 1980

76

Hoyt Vincent Nordeman

Hoyt Vincent   Dorothy Breidenthal
B. Jan. 7, 1891   B. Apr. 15, 1893
D. Dec. 2, 1951   D. Apr. 1973

Their first three children were Hoyt Vincent Jr., Kenneth Warren and Dorothy Lydia May (always referred to as Sister). In 1931, a second daughter, Eunice Jean was born.

Four generations are pictured here. Charles L. Dow is holding
Hoyt V. Nordeman, Jr. Hoyt V. Nordeman, Sr. and his mother
Ednah Dow Nordeman look on. The picture was taken in 1914

Dorothy and Hoyt Nordeman with their family

From left to right in foreground

Kenneth Warren	Dorothy Lydia May	Hoyt Vincent Jr.
B. May 31, 1916	B. Feb. 18, 1918	B. Nov. 3, 1913
D. Aug. 20, 1981	D. Nov. 10, 1969	D. Oct. 2, 1964

Eunice Jean (not pictured)
B. Sep. 17, 1931
D.

Made in the USA
Charleston, SC
09 February 2013